CAN-AM COMPETITION

World's Fastest Sports Car Racing

CAN-AM COMPETITION

World's Fastest Sports Car Racing

by Robert B. Jackson

illustrated with photographs

New York / *Henry Z. Walck. Inc.*

629.22   Jackson, Robert B.
  J   Can-Am, world's fastest road racing.
         Walck, 1972
            64p. illus.

            An account of the Canadian-American
         Challenge Cup races, the drivers, and
         their cars.

            1. Automobile racing   2. Canadian-Am-
         erican Challenge Cup   I. Title

THE PHOTOGRAPHS OF THE 2J CHAPARRAL ON PAGE 49 WERE KINDLY
SUPPLIED BY BOB KELLY, PRESS DIRECTOR OF THE WATKINS GLEN
GRAND PRIX CORPORATION. THE PHOTOGRAPH OF THE 1971 ROAD
ATLANTA, GEORGIA, CAN-AM RACE BY DOZIER MOBLEY ON PAGE 59 IS
REPRODUCED THROUGH THE COURTESY OF DAVE HOUSER, PUBLIC RELA-
TIONS DIRECTOR FOR ROAD ATLANTA. OTHER PHOTOGRAPHS ARE BY
THE AUTHOR.

22494

Contents

1 / *Champagne Peter*

THE PUMPKIN-COLORED McLAREN sped into the turn, squeezed past several cars it was lapping, and then howled up the long hill. Following the curves as precisely as an oversized slot-car and skimming down the straights at two hundred miles an hour, the big sports/racer thundered through its final lap.

When it streaked past the starter's waving checkered flag, the British automobile had easily won another important Can-Am race, just as Team McLaren cars had done so often in the past. The difference this time, however, was that an American sat in the low cockpit of the fast racer.

Young Peter Revson, who had started his driving career as an amateur with the Sports Car Club of

America and then gone to Europe to gain experience, was now an established professional in the United States and in his first season with the McLaren Can-Am team. Although Peter had been driving in the Canadian-American Challenge Cup series of road races since its beginning, this was the first year that he had been behind the wheel of a truly competitive car and he was making the most of it.

While he slowly toured the course on a cool-off lap, he removed his helmet and protective cloth driving hood, then wiped his brow with the back of his forearm. The large crowds jamming the fences cheered noisily when the victorious McLaren passed; and Peter waved happily in return.

Still soaked with perspiration, he scrambled from the car at the start-finish line and was immediately surrounded by a cluster of questioning newsmen and jostling photographers. The crush about him continued to grow as Peter was hoisted to a nearby platform where he received the usual wreath of laurel leaves and kiss from the race queen.

The final award was a silver trophy bowl which was presented to Peter and then filled with the traditional champagne. He hoisted the brimming bowl to his mouth to drink a few customary swallows, drenching the front of his driving suit as he did so. All the while clamoring photographers kept insisting that every action be repeated in each direction for them all to get a good shot; and next they asked Peter to hold the trophy high in the air for still more pictures.

Yielding to the elation of his victory, the jubilant driver poured the bowl of sparkling wine over the head of a nearby television interviewer instead. While the announcer was still sputtering, Peter took the big bottle itself, shook it violently, and gleefully sprayed spurting champagne over everyone else he could reach, with particular attention to the photographers.

From then on he was often referred to as "Champagne Peter" in the automobile racing columns. By the

"Champagne Peter" Revson celebrates a 1971 Can-Am victory.

time the 1971 Canadian-American Challenge Cup series ended, he had earned a far more important title, however. Peter won a total of five Can-Ams that season and became the 1971 Can-Am driving champion, the first American ever to hold the title.

2 / *The Most Powerful Cars on the Road*

HELD ANNUALLY between June and October, the Canadian-American Challenge Cup series consists of some seven two-hundred-mile road races in the United States and two or three similar events in Canada. These ten or so professional races are run under international rules determined by the Fédération Internationale de l'Automobile in Paris and are organized by the Sports Car Club of America, assisted by the Canadian Automobile Sports Clubs. The Can-Am, which offers a total of more than a million dollars in prizes, is the richest series of road races in the world; and each season it attracts the best drivers and cars from many countries.

Can-Am cars are what the Sports Car Club of America calls sports/racers. In spite of the first part of this name, however, they have little in common with production sports cars such as the Triumphs and Datsuns you see on the street. Like sports cars, they are required to have enclosed wheels, doors and a passenger seat, it is true. This distinguishes them from open-wheeled single-seater formula cars.

But the emphasis of sports/racing cars is very much on the second part of their name. Can-Am builders give little attention to such "street" considerations as comfort, durability or cost of operation, their major concern being pure speed.

First of all, Can-Am racers differ from the majority of street sports cars in general layout. The usual order from the front of most production sports cars (as well as family automobiles) is engine, transmission and passenger area. In contrast the large engine of a Can-Am sports/racer is located just behind the open cockpit; and its gearbox is attached to the engine at the rear of the car. This arrangement gives better weight distribution and improves the car's handling.

In addition, the dramatically styled body of a Can-Am car is unlike anything you might see on the highway, sweeping up from a chisel-shaped nose to form a low wedge that looks fast even when it is not in motion. Can-Am tires are also much wider than street versions for better road holding, the "steamroller" rears on some

This wedge-shaped McLaren M8F has body-long stabilizing fins that sweep up to support the "Batmobile" wing. The air duct that leads to the opening near the car's number helps to cool the engine.

cars now measuring a foot and a half across the tread. And even more startling in appearance is the stubby wing mounted at the rear of a Can-Am competitor. This wing presses the car down on the road and prevents it from lifting at high speeds like an airplane.

Can-Am bodies are also more advanced than those of sports cars in having streamlined channels that guide air to several openings of varying size. Some of these

/ 13

ducts assist in cooling operating parts such as the engine and brakes while others use the force of entering air to help keep the car from becoming airborne. Projecting fins, called spoilers or fences, are also attached at several points on the car to direct the flow of air about the body and make the vehicle more stable.

The internal design of Can-Am cars is even more unusual. Instead of having a heavy steel frame to which the other parts are bolted, as in a conventional automobile, the typical Can-Am chassis is basically a series of connected aluminum boxes. This "monocoque" chassis, much lighter and stronger than a conventional frame-type, is built on the principle of an eggshell. The aluminum skin of a Can-Am chassis not only takes the major stresses acting on the car, it also acts as part of the body in a great saving of weight.

Similar concentration on weight reduction is seen everywhere else in Can-Am cars as well. This is because, other things being equal, the lighter a car is, the faster it will go. Extremely light metal alloys that were originally developed for spacecraft are used extensively in Can-Am construction, for instance; and the thin plastic upper-body shells have their color cast in to save the weight of paint. Even the engines have aluminum blocks instead of cast-iron blocks like those of street cars.

The engines of Can-Am cars are generally made to

save weight in another way, also. The engine of a sports car in everyday use is mounted on its chassis but remains structurally separate from it. In a Can-Am racer, however, the engine is bolted to the end of the monocoque "tub" and itself forms the rear portion of the frame with the rear suspension being attached directly to it.

As a result of these advanced design and construction methods, Can-Am cars are feather-light for their size. A McLaren M8F weighs approximately 1500 pounds; but in comparison a Corvette, which has the same wheelbase, weighs about 3300 pounds, more than twice as much.

Can-Am designers economize on space as well as weight by such techniques as using the interior of their monocoque chassis to contain several rubber bags for fuel. Since a thirsty Can-Am engine uses about a gallon of gasoline every three miles, seventy gallons or so are needed for the usual two-hundred-mile event; and much of the chassis is therefore filled with gasoline at the start of a race.

The Fédération Internationale de l'Automobile requires that these fuel bags be made of a puncture-resistant material and that they be filled with a sponge-like plastic foam to prevent the gasoline from spilling out in an accident and possibly catching fire. The international rules also specify that a Can-Am car must

A McLaren M8A with its two body panels and front wheels removed. The large hoses either side of the gearbox direct air to the rear brakes.

have a strong roll bar, two independent braking systems, a built-in fire extinguisher, and a safety harness for the driver that is attached to the car at six points.

Other than these stringent safety requirements, the FIA has placed unusually few restrictions on Can-Am design. The cockpits must be forty inches wide, the engines have to be at least 153 cubic inches in size, no gas turbines are allowed—and that's about it. Since neither a maximum engine size nor a weight minimum is specified, giant engines are stuffed into unusually light chassis; and this has been the largest factor in making Can-Am cars so blindingly fast.

Special European racing engines have been used in some Can-Am cars; but, advanced as they are, they have not been as successful as modified versions of U.S. production engines. While the small European racing engines produce more power for their size, the much larger U.S. engines turn out far more power overall. Therefore cars with U.S. engines have won forty-eight of the forty-nine Can-Am races held through the end of the 1971 season for a nearly perfect record. In an even more astonishing sweep, Chevrolet V-8's accounted for forty-seven of the forty-eight victories.

These Can-Am Chevrolets are much different from the mass-produced engines that sit under the hoods of family Chevvies, of course. Their blocks, heads, valves and crankshafts were originally high-performance Corvette options; but they have been skillfully reworked and painstakingly combined with many special new parts to produce much greater power. Again using a street Corvette for comparison, its standard engine has a 350-inch displacement and achieves two hundred horsepower. The largest Can-Am Chevrolets are currently an

Modified Chevrolet V-8 engines have powered all but two Can-Am winners. The eight mushroom-like objects are ram-pipes for air, fuel being injected at their bases. (When the engine is not running it is kept clean by covering the ends of the ram-pipes with plastic kitchen-bowl covers.)

enormous 510 cubic inches in size and crank out more than 750 horsepower. They also cost as much as thirteen thousand dollars, more than twice the price of an entire Corvette.

Although U.S. engines have performed remarkably well in the first six years of Can-Am racing, U.S. chassis have done poorly, winning only a single race. It has been an international combination of a powerful U.S. engine in a road-hugging British chassis that has dominated Can-Am competition thus far. A Lola-Ford has won one race, Lola-Chevrolets have won seven, and the highly successful McLaren-Chevrolets have won no less than thirty-nine.

Can-Am cars such as the latest Lolas and McLarens are incredibly fast, exceeding one hundred miles an hour in bottom gear alone and easily topping two hundred miles an hour on long straights. As someone once said, they are dragsters that steer better.

Equally important for road racing, the brakes of Can-Am cars are as good as their acceleration. A typical Can-Am sports/racer can drag away from a stop, reach one hundred miles an hour, and come to a stop again, all within less than ten seconds.

Such performance has caused road racing fans to compare the average speeds of the unlimited Can-Am competitors to those of Grand Prix cars, the acknowledged aristocrats of motor sport. Single-seater Grand Prix open-wheelers are the most advanced cars in the world technically; they also have the advantages of being lighter and offering less resistance to the air than the larger Can-Am cars.

But the FIA currently limits GP engines to a maximum of three liters, or only 183 cubic inches; and this handicaps the Grand Prix cars by a couple of hundred horsepower on long straights. On the other hand, the thoroughbred Grand Prix automobiles are faster in the turns where top speed is not as important.

On courses with long straights, Can-Am cars are therefore slightly faster; but a twisty circuit gives the edge to Grand Prix automobiles. In any case, the best lap speeds of the quickest cars of both types are very close, averaging out to within a mile or two of each other.

There is no question that Can-Am sports/racers have much the better of GP cars in sheer power, however. And when their big bellowing engines push the Can-Am giants down the straights at speeds just a shade slower than greased lightning, there are many fans who will say that Can-Am cars surpass Grand Prix automobiles in dramatic effect, too.

3 / Can-Am Competition

ROAD RACING first became widespread in this country just after World War II as amateur competition; but eventually the sport attracted so much interest that professional events were added to the schedule. The Sports Car Club of America, which had organized the first important amateur races, started an annual international endurance event at Sebring, Florida; and the United States Automobile Club sanctioned several early professional meets, beginning in 1958.

After these pioneer pro races had proved highly popular with both competitors and spectators, the SCCA went a step further. In 1963 it undertook a nationwide, season-long series of professional races called the United States Road Racing Championship. Unlike the SCCA's amateur program, which stressed production sports car racing, the USRRC was open only to sports/racing cars, called "modified sports cars" in those days.

Important in its own right, the USRRC also turned out to be a training ground for the Can-Am which succeeded it. Many U.S. drivers, designers, mechanics, reporters and spectators first learned about big-time sports car competition from USRRC racing. Then, when the more ambitious Canadian-American Challenge Cup series was announced for the season of 1966, they were enthusiastically ready.

The Can-Am was major-league road racing from the very beginning, offering substantial sums of money as prizes and drawing top-ranked competitors from both sides of the Atlantic. It did start as a short fall series of only six races, however.

This was to avoid conflict with the USRRC, which continued as a championship of considerably lessened importance until it was finally discontinued after the season of 1968. Another reason for first holding the Can-Am series in September, October and November was to incorporate several already popular races that were traditionally run in those months. The fall schedule was also intended to attract the European drivers whose season elsewhere was quiet at that time of year.

The first Can-Am race took place on September 11,

Can-Am racing was major league competition from its beginning. Shown here are the McLaren team (cars 5 and 4) and Dan Gurney in a Lola (36) making a flying start at Bridgehampton, New York, in 1967.

1966, on Le Circuit Mont Tremblant in St. Jovite, Quebec, two hours northwest of Montreal, in the beautiful Laurentian Mountains. An intense, graying British driver, John Surtees, won the inaugural in a swift Lola T70-Chevrolet. Surtees, a motorcycle-racing champion seven times before turning to automobiles, had been

World Champion in 1964 driving Grand Prix cars for Ferrari, and was now running his own Can-Am team.

Second and third in that first Can-Am race were two young New Zealanders, Bruce McLaren and Chris Amon driving a pair of Bruce's new sports/racers. This dropped a strong hint as to the future of the series as did the fact that Chuck Parsons, the USRRC champion that season, finished sixth, two laps behind. The McLaren team was to dominate the Can-Am in later seasons; and with few exceptions, American drivers would be outclassed for some time.

During practice for the first Can-Am race, two Lolas lifted their noses while cresting over a rise at about one hundred and thirty miles an hour. Airborne and without steering, they leaped upwards and then fell back upside down in what is called the "speedboat effect." Fortunately there were no injuries in either accident; but the flips were a serious indication of the handling difficulties caused by the continually increasing speeds of the unlimited sports/racers. The big cars have become so fast they act like planes under certain conditions; and one of the biggest concerns of Can-Am designers has been to learn how the air resists the passage of their cars at high speed in order to make them controllable at all times.

One of the first to put a new idea into practice was

Jim Hall, Texas millionaire and creator of the revolutionary Chaparral racing cars.

Jim Hall, builder and a driver of the revolutionary Chaparrals. Hall's white speedsters had overpowered the USRRC during 1964 and 1965; and a Chaparral had astonished the European teams by beating them at their own game on the demanding Nürburgring in Germany during the spring of 1966.

Hall, a Texas oilman when he is not racing, was

already widely known in 1966 for such original ideas as using automatic transmissions in his Chaparrals and constructing their monocoque chassis from plastic. Even more radical developments were yet to come from the shops at Hall's Rattlesnake Raceway, however.

His new Chaparral 2E's had not been ready for the 1966 St. Jovite Can-Am opener; but a pair of the cars arrived at the sandy seaside paddock at Bridgehampton, New York, for the second race of the series. They immediately caused a furor; and everyone came running for a closer look at the 2E's, even before they were off their trailers.

To begin with, an air-scooped water radiator bulged from the front of each rear fender. This unfamiliar location not only gave better cooling for the engine, it made the 2E's faster. Without the conventional radiator at its front, a 2E had a much sharper nose than its rivals and thus encountered less air resistance.

Startling as these fender radiators were, what really had most observers open-mouthed were the big wings perched on slim struts three feet above the rear of the 2E's. Similar wings have since become standard equipment on the fastest sports and formula cars to help keep them on the road; but Hall's "flippers" were the first public appearance of such a device and they created a sensation.

The radical 2E Chaparral featured rear-mounted radiators and a high movable wing.

The wing of a 2E was controlled from the cockpit to tilt in the turns and exert a stronger downforce on the suspension there. The same foot control also pivoted a flap within the nose to regulate airflow through the car and further increase stability. This system proved to be highly effective at Bridgehampton; and Hall lowered the previous lap record there by nearly six seconds to qualify for the pole position at the start.

The driver of the second 2E was Phil Hill, co-winner at the Nürburgring in the 2D Chaparral that spring and the only U.S. driver ever to have been World Champion (1961). When Jim's car had wing trouble in late practice, went off the road, and was damaged too badly to repair in time for the race, Phil then became the only Chaparral entry. He was very much in contention during most of the event, running a close second for fifty laps; but his wing-control failed near the end of the race and he had to settle for fourth.

The winner, who led from start to finish in a dark blue 305-cubic-inch Lola-Ford, was rangy Californian Dan Gurney. Dan had been successful at driving everything from stock cars to Grand Prix automobiles in a widely varied racing career; and his Long Island victory

Dan Gurney's Can-Am victory at Bridgehampton in 1966 was a popular one. His car is a Lola-Ford.

was a popular one because he was a particular favorite of many of the fans. (The occasion was also memorable in that it was the only Can-Am race to date won by a Ford engine.) Less than a car-length behind Dan at the checker was a charging Chris Amon, and Bruce McLaren followed for third.

The third race of that first Can-Am season was run the following week at Mosport (for "motor sport") Park near Ontario; and a most exciting contest it was. The Lola of John Surtees and three other cars were eliminated in a dusty, spinning collision in the first turn of the first lap; and the pace then became so rapid that fifteen other drivers (including Bruce McLaren and Jim Hall) had to drop out at later stages.

With only ten laps left to go Dan Gurney's second Can-Am victory in a row seemed likely; but the ignition system of his Lola suddenly failed, and he dejectedly coasted to a stop as the rest of the field sped past. Inheriting first place and holding on to win was a rosy-cheeked engineer with a crewcut driving a Lola T70 in his first season with a new team from Philadelphia.

In those days the now-famous Mark Donohue was a recent graduate from amateur SCCA ranks. Similarly, team owner-manager Roger Penske had only recently retired from driving to manage his first big-time racing team. The pair were eventually to collect many more victories in several different types of competition and become the talk of the racing world.

The inaugural Can-Am series next moved to the West Coast for the second half of the season. Phil Hill and Jim Hall swept the Laguna Seca, California, race in the winged 2E Chaparrals, taking first and second easily, with Bruce McLaren third and Mark Donohue fourth.

In contrast, the fifth race of 1966, held at hot Riverside Raceway near Los Angeles, was anything but a runaway. Bruce McLaren took an early lead, then had to give way to Jim Hall, who, in turn, was tightly pressed by John Surtees. Hall in the Chaparral and Surtees in the Lola swapped the lead five times in the next twenty-two laps, Surtees finally crossing the finish-line first when Hall was slowed by a partial fuel-blockage during the last few minutes.

John Surtees and Phil Hill were now tied for 1966 Can-Am championship points with only the Las Vegas race left on the schedule. Although Jim Hall and Phil were able to qualify fastest in their 2E's on the desert, both had problems with their wings during the race. John Surtees then sped to another victory, setting the highest average speed of the series that year, 109.25 mph, and winning the first Can-Am championship.

Bruce McLaren came in second at Las Vegas, plac-

Can-Am champion in 1966, Briton John Surtees now concentrates on Grand Prix racing.

ing third in the overall championship; and steady Mark Donohue finished third in the final event which gave him second place in the championship standings. Fourth at Nevada, but well down in the final point-list tied for tenth, was another young driver who had been Mark Donohue's chief SCCA rival, Peter Revson.

4 / *The Orange Train*

SHORT, QUIET and nearly always smiling when he was
out of the cockpit, the late Bruce McLaren was one of
the most likable of racing drivers and a perfectionist
about the automobiles he built. Following in his father's
footsteps (or perhaps more accurately in his tire tracks),
Bruce started racing automobiles in his native New
Zealand when he was a teen-ager. He did so well there
that he was sent to England on a racing "scholarship" by
the New Zealand Grand Prix Association to compete in
European formula races.

Driving for the English Cooper team behind Aus-
tralian "Black Jack" Brabham, World Champion with
Cooper in 1959 and 1960, Bruce won the first United
States Grand Prix at Sebring, Florida, at the age of only

New Zealander Bruce McLaren, whose exceptional sports/racers have dominated Can-Am competition.

twenty-two. When Brabham left Cooper to start his own racing organization, Bruce then became Cooper's Number One driver.

In turn Bruce also left Cooper to form his own team which eventually was to build, race, and also sell Grand Prix, Formula 5000 (Continental) and Can-Am cars.

Already a good driver, Bruce became an even better car-builder and businessman; and his exceptional Can-Am sports/racers were his greatest achievement.

His close involvement with big sports cars began in the days Bruce was with Cooper and bought an unusual vehicle called the Zerex Special. This was a 1961 Grand Prix Cooper that had been wrecked at the United States Grand Prix and later rebuilt with a new body as a sports/racer by Roger Penske. Bruce bought the car in 1964 and made his own modifications, including the installation of an Oldsmobile engine.

Based on what Bruce and his new team learned from racing the Zerex Special, they built the M1A McLaren, first of the long line of speedy sports/racers to bear his name. After competing with M1A's in Europe and the U.S. during 1964 and 1965, the McLaren team next produced an improved version, the M1B. It was a two-car team of M1B's that Bruce ran in the first Can-Am series of 1966.

The McLaren organization, an English-American group directed by Philadelphian Teddy Mayer with Tyler Alexander from Massachusetts as chief mechanic, then built three new cars, the M6A's, for the 1967 Can-Am. The fastest McLarens yet, they were the first monocoque McLaren sports cars and the first of the line to bear the familiar pumpkin-orange color.

Like all Can-Am McLarens, the M6A represented gradual improvement, simplification and increased reliability rather than radical change.

The M6A's owed much to the earlier McLaren sports/racers, of course; but many ideas from the team's Grand Prix cars had also been included in their design. As with all Can-Am McLarens, the emphasis was on gradual improvement, simplification and increased reliability rather than radical change.

There was a new driver on the team for 1967, as Denny Hulme, another New Zealander, joined Bruce. Denny is a balding, happy-go-lucky individual known for racing in his bare feet during his younger days at home. In 1967 he also drove a Grand Prix car for Jack Brabham and became World Champion.

It has always been a characteristic of the McLaren operation that their cars receive lengthy and careful

Denny Hulme, World Champion in 1967 and Can-Am champion in both 1968 and 1970. He is often called "The Big Bear."

testing. The first M6A, for example, was completed three months before the opening Can-Am race of 1967 and had already undergone more than 2,000 miles of testing when the team arrived at the scenic Road America course in Elkhart Lake, Wisconsin, to open the season.

In contrast, the opposing teams were not nearly as well prepared and were still making corrections on their cars during practice. The McLaren drivers were thus able to outqualify them for the first two starting positions, Denny lopping almost ten seconds off the previous lap record and Bruce qualifying a tenth of a second faster. When Bruce had to drop out with an oil leak, it was Denny who won the race, leading the thirty-two-car field from flag to flag and lapping all but two in the process.

Once established, this marked superiority of the McLaren team was to last throughout the 1967 season. Denny and Bruce finished in 1-2 order at both Bridgehampton and Mosport; and Bruce won at Laguna Seca and Riverside. The only non-McLaren victory of the series came at Las Vegas when Denny had a flat tire and Bruce's engine went sour. John Surtees then won the closing race of the series for the second year in a row.

The McLaren team compiled a Can-Am record in 1967 of five victories in six races, five of six pole positions and the fastest lap in all six events. This easily gave the overall championship to Bruce and second place to Denny.

By now the other Can-Am competitors were so impressed by the speed and reliability of the McLaren M6A's that Bruce was able to sell a number of produc-

The Roger Penske "customer" M6B McLaren of 1968 with Mark Donohue at the wheel.

tion versions, called M6B's, to his opposition. One of his customers was Roger Penske who bought an M6B which he lightened and modified for Mark Donohue. Mark and Roger not only won the 1968 USRRC, for the second season in a row, with the M6B, they also used the series to improve the car for the more demanding Can-Am championship that followed in the fall.

Dan Gurney also bought an M6B from the Mc-

Laren team for 1968 and his All American Racers team rebuilt it, using many construction methods from their own "Eagle" Indianapolis and Grand Prix cars. For this reason, the Gurney M6B was often called a "McLeagle." The car was originally powered by a Ford engine; and a Chevrolet was tried later in its career as well. The "McLeagle" was also rebuilt at one point using rare, super-light and ultra-expensive metals; but in spite of these and other changes, the car was never really competitive.

Several other Can-Am teams, including that of John Surtees, chose to race the new Lola T160 during 1968. Jim Hall stayed with his year-old 2G Chaparral because the new 2H was not yet running well; and a flame-red Ferrari V-12 sports/racer was air-freighted from Italy to Las Vegas for the last race of the championship. (Unlike the endurance-type Ferraris that had run three Can-Am races the previous year, this 612 Ferrari was built just for the two-hour Can-Am events and had the largest Ferrari engine ever made, 380 cubic inches.)

But none of these cars, the M6B "customer" McLarens included, was fast enough to keep up with the 1968 McLaren team entries, the new M8A's. Among other advances, these latest team McLarens had a revised body shape that was "chopped" vertically at the tail to reduce lift. The M8A's also had new 427-inch aluminum Chevrolet engines of 620 horsepower, one hundred more

Peter Revson drove a McLaren M6B for Carroll Shelby, builder of the famous Cobras, in 1968.

than the 358-inch cast-iron McLaren Chevvies of the previous season. These improvements plus the group's extremely high standards of workmanship and preparation made the bright orange M8A's almost impossible to catch, much less defeat.

Bruce opened the 1968 season by slicing three seconds from his 1967 qualifying record at Road America to take the pole; and Denny, only a tenth of a second slower, was right behind him on the grid. Although Jim Hall's 2G was in third starting position, Jim was a full second slower than Bruce; and the two team McLarens proceeded to run away with the race, Denny finishing first and Bruce second.

The "Bruce and Denny Show," as it came to be called, continued to demoralize the opposition throughout the 1968 season. Jim Hall did push the pair so hard

The "Bruce and Denny Show" (between them chief mechanic Tyler Alexander) monopolized first and second places in Can-Am races from 1967 until 1970.

at Bridgehampton that their engines "blew"; but in doing so he only helped Mark Donohue to victory because the Chaparral's engine, overstressed in the chase, eventually lost power. And John Cannon won at Laguna Seca in an old McLaren 1B when a driving rainstorm caught the tire company supplying the McLaren team without the proper rain tires.

Other than these two losses, however, Bruce and Denny outclassed the field again in 1968, Denny winning the championship and Bruce coming in second to reverse the order of their 1967 finish. The pattern of their qualifying for the first two grid positions and one following the other to the checkered flag had now become well established; and their competitors continued to marvel at the speed and strength of their cars. It was for these reasons that Stirling Moss, the famous retired British racing driver, called Team McLaren the "Orange Train."

5 / *Million Dollar Racing*

ATTRACTING many more spectators with each season, the Can-Am was expanded from six to eleven races in 1969. Such courses as Watkins Glen, New York, Mid-Ohio at Lexington, Ohio, and Edmonton, Alberta, were added to the schedule to make a season-long championship from the original fall series.

The amount of prize money was also boosted considerably at this time. A total of $550,000 was posted for 1969 race purses, and an additional fund of $200,000 was set aside for division among the ten top point-winners at the end of the season. (Can-Am points are now awarded on a 20-15-12-10-8-6-4-3-2-1 basis after each race.)

When the approximately $200,000 in awards from

manufacturers of automotive products was added to the purse and championship funds, the total prize money for 1969 reached nearly a million dollars. (The overall amount has increased even more since then and now exceeds the million mark, making the Can-Am by far the richest series in road racing.)

Several teams hoped to challenge the McLaren organization for the greatly increased awards of 1969; and among them was Jim Hall, who had a new Chaparral, the 2H coupe. The 2H was much narrower than other Can-Am cars, and had a slippery fishlike shape so low at the cockpit that the driver's head projected through an opening in the roof and the side windows were at his elbows. The new Chaparral also had an unusual rear suspension with road-grabbing tires that were nearly two feet wide. Because Hall was still recovering from injuries he had received in a bad crash at the end of the 1968 season, he hired John Surtees, Can-Am champion in 1966, to drive the 2H.

Charley Parsons had the latest Lola T162 in 1969; Chris Amon returned in a rebodied 612 Ferrari; and Swiss star Jo Siffert ran several of the races in a modified German Porsche endurance-type 917 sports car. The McLaren customers also had their M12's, production versions of the highly successful team M8A's of the previous season. It was the same old story, however, as none of them was good enough to beat the McLaren team.

Bruce and Denny remained a jump ahead of their opposition by fielding a pair of improved M8B McLarens. The new team cars were recognizable by the wing at the back (the first for a Can-Am McLaren) and deep air-scoops at the rear of the front wheel-wells which cooled the brakes.

They could also be identified as the cars that won *all* eleven Can-Am races in 1969 and took eight second places as well. Bruce became Can-Am champion for the second time by winning six events; and Denny was second in the overall standings with five. Everyone else was so far down on the list in total points as to be out of sight.

A telling example of the complete McLaren mastery during 1969 occurred at Bridgehampton out on Long Island. Bruce and Denny were able to set qualifying times seconds faster than anyone else by lunchtime of practice day. That afternoon, while the other teams were still trying to equal their speed, Bruce and Denny went water-skiing on Peconic Bay. When they returned to race the following day, Denny won without difficulty, raising the record average speed to 113.7 mph. Bruce finished second, only a tenth of a second behind.

Many long hours of hard work behind the scenes

Bruce, here pushing his car to the starting grid, became Can-Am champion for the second time in 1969.

were needed to keep the McLaren Can-Am cars so far in front of the other teams, of course. At the same time, the McLaren organization was also deeply involved in Grand Prix racing, and—after 1969—in preparing for the Indianapolis 500 as well. Bruce was thus kept very busy supervising three major racing programs; but he still preferred to do as much testing of the new cars himself as he could.

In early June of 1970 Bruce took a new Can-Am M8D down to the Goodwood circuit in Sussex to check it out for the forthcoming season. Lighter than earlier McLarens and with an even larger 465 cubic-inch engine, the M8D also had a revised wing arrangement to conform with new FIA regulations.

The fragilely strutted wings that pushed directly on rear suspensions, first introduced by Jim Hall, had been widely copied by racing car designers, including those of Grand Prix automobiles. But after several GP cars crashed badly when their wing supports broke and changed the cars' handling drastically, the FIA required that all wings be an integral part of the bodywork as a safety measure.

In compliance with the new rule, the wing of the M8D was supported between the trailing ends of a pair of angular fins that rose sharply from the sides of the car. The strange appearance of this unusual design soon earned the nickname of "Batmobile" for the M8D.

While testing various angles of the new wing, Bruce turned a lap of over 122 miles an hour and then came in for a suspension adjustment. He was back out on the course a few laps later when the rear bodywork of the car lifted from the chassis just as he was coming out of a turn at 170. Because its wing was no longer functional, the car swerved out of control immediately and smashed into a banking, killing Bruce.

The entire racing world was shocked and grieved by the terrible accident, of course; and the McLaren team was naturally most shaken of all. They decided to continue racing without their leader, however; and Dan Gurney became their second driver for the early races of the 1970 season.

Dan won the Mosport opener and also the St. Jovite race two weeks later, extending the long series of McLaren victories. But when the Can-Am circus arrived at Watkins Glen in July for the third race in 1970, there was a great surprise for everyone. Jim Hall turned up there with his latest white Chaparral, the 2J; and once again its design was revolutionary.

In addition to the big 465 Chevrolet engine behind the driver that moved the car, the 2J also had a snow-mobile-type engine in its extreme rear. This extra engine drove two fans that pulled air from beneath the sports/racer much like a vacuum cleaner. Flexible plastic skirts attached to the bottom of the car reached to within a quarter-inch of the road and sealed off the area beneath the 2J, permitting a partial vacuum to develop there.

The vacuum literally sucked the moving car to the road and vastly improved its braking, acceleration and

Most radical of all Jim Hall's unusual Chaparrals, the 2J was said to resemble the box it came in. Visible in the rear view are the two fans that created suction beneath the car to improve its road holding.

especially its cornering. The system was so powerful that the 2J could be driven upside down across a ceiling! Little wonder that members of other teams surrounded the car at Watkins Glen, slowly shaking their heads in disbelief.

With the pair of fans extending from the rear of the 2J and its straight, angular shape that allowed it to be "sealed" to the road, the 2J appeared ugly to many observers. In fact, a joke circulated up and down the pit lane that the 2J looked like the box it came in.

The driver Jim Hall secured to test the radical 2J at Watkins Glen was certainly no joke, however. He was the little mod Scot, Jackie Stewart, World Champion in 1969 and 1971. Famous for the burr in his voice, his shoulder-length hair and little black cap, Jackie is generally acknowledged to be the best race driver since Jimmy Clark.

Jackie was able to put the 2J in third grid position; and he also turned the fastest lap of the race, considerable accomplishments for a highly experimental car its first time in competition. The "sucker car" did have to retire part way through the race with mechanical problems, though; and Denny Hulme won still another race for McLaren.

The 2J Chaparral missed the next two races while it was being revised; and Denny collected further victo-

Jackie Stewart, the best racing driver of his time.

ries at Edmonton, Alberta, and Mid-Ohio. By this time
Dan Gurney had been forced to leave the McLaren team
because of a sponsorship conflict; and Peter Gethin had
come over from England to replace him. In only his
third Can-Am race, Gethin was declared the winner at
Road America after Denny was disqualified for a push-
start following a spin.

The 2J "vacuum cleaner" returned to competition at

the inaugural Can-Am race held on the beautiful rolling Road Atlanta course in Georgia. Rebuilt since Watkins Glen, the improved Chaparral was now driven by British rally-expert Vic Elford; and it proved to be unquestionably faster than the McLarens at Road Atlanta. In an upset that rated headlines in the sports pages, Elford qualified on the pole 1.26 seconds faster than Denny, the first time in three years that a McLaren was not on the pole for a Can-Am start.

That Road Atlanta Can-Am of 1970 turned out to be one of the most unusual races of the series in other ways as well, resembling a demolition derby at times. While holding an early lead Denny Hulme hit a car he was lapping and had to drop out; the 2J failed to live up to its qualifying promise, pitting with fan-motor trouble; and Peter Gethin, who took over the lead from Denny, crushed the nose of his M8D "Batmobile" when he spun.

All these retirements left Peter Revson and his Lola T220 in first place—until a tire blew, sending Peter into a banking. Directly behind Peter at that moment was the ex-Dan Gurney "McLeagle" now driven by Bob Brown, which inherited the lead in turn, but only for a split second. Brown was blinded by the dust of Revson's collision and he crashed into the rear of the stalled Lola, neither driver being hurt.

The new leader then became the young Canadian

department-store heir, George Eaton, who was driving a BRM (British Racing Motors) P154. Eaton's engine faltered after nineteen more laps, however, and Peter Gethin, the nose of his M8D repaired by fast pitwork, regained first place for what finally appeared to be a certain victory.

But when Gethin's gearbox developed problems and he, too, had to quit, the surprising winner of the incident-filled race became Briton Tony Dean in his Porsche 908 Spyder, a car with an engine less than half the size of the big Chevrolets. This was the first non-McLaren Can-Am victory since John Surtees won in a Lola at Las Vegas in 1967. It is also the only time a non-American engine has powered a Can-Am winner to date.

The boxy but fast 2J Chaparral was most impressive again while practicing for the two big West Coast races that end the Can-Am schedule. At both Laguna Seca and Riverside in 1970 the 2J qualified on the pole approximately two seconds faster than the McLarens. But its engine blew just before the Laguna Seca race, and the fan motor failed at Riverside. Denny then breezed to two more McLaren victories, giving him a total of six in the 1970 series and his second Can-Am championship.

Placing second in the 1970 point-totals was independent McLaren driver Lothar Motschenbacher. The

German-born former Mercedes-Benz mechanic had won thirty-two formula races before turning to Can-Am competition. Lothar is typical of the lesser-publicized private drivers who make up the larger part of any Can-Am starting grid in that he must compete with a smaller racing budget and less technical help than the "factory" teams. On the other hand, he is unusual in being the only driver, factory or private, to have raced in every Can-Am event thus far.

6 / *Revvie and the Big Bear*

BEFORE the sixth Can-Am season began in 1971, the FIA had arrived at a decision that still has road racing fans arguing with each other. The world body ruled that vacuum cars, such as Jim Hall's 2J Chaparral, have an unfair advantage over other competitors and that the 2J and similar automobiles could not race in international events.

The other teams were relieved to hear that the 2J had been banned because it meant they did not have to develop expensive vacuum systems of their own to remain competitive. In opposition to this point of view, Hall and his many disappointed fans thought the FIA had been too conservative in outlawing a valuable advance in racing-car design; and the controversy has continued until the present.

Notice the anti-lift holes in the blunt nose of the Lola T260. In spite of many such consultations between Jackie Stewart and the rest of the team during practice sessions in 1971, the car never really handled well.

Once the "sucker car" had been legislated back to its garage in Texas, the next serious challenge to Mc-Laren supremacy came from the more conventional Lola T260. Blunt-nosed and boxy in comparison to the Mc-

Larens, the red-striped white T260 was also two and one-half feet shorter than an M8F. But the most unusual feature of the compact T260 to the casual eye was the many small holes dotting its nose. They were intended to allow the escape of air from the inside at speed to reduce lift.

With the heavy financial backing of a cigarette manufacturer, a tire company and an oil supplier among others, the Lola campaign of 1971 was planned as an all-out effort at finally ending the McLaren dynasty. To this end Jackie Stewart was selected to drive the T260.

Jackie and the single Lola were pitted against a McLaren team of two M8F's, further-improved offspring of the M8D "Batmobiles." As in 1970, the team's senior driver was bluff and hearty Denny Hulme, who is often called "The Big Bear" by other drivers. The second M8F was entrusted to a new team-member, young Peter Revson.

"Revvie," who comes from a very wealthy family, first raced as an amateur in SCCA production cars. He later went to Europe for experience in single-seater racing, usually driving his own car on a shoestring budget. Peter had also driven in the Can-Am for at least part of every season since its beginning, becoming faster and smoother each year.

He first met McLaren team manager Teddy Mayer

at Cornell University when they were both involved in SCCA racing there. Then, in 1970 Peter took over a track-racing McLaren from Chris Amon for the tough Indianapolis 500 and impressed the McLaren group very favorably in his first drive for them.

They signed him to compete for Team McLaren in Indianapolis-type racing for the rest of the 1970 season and for both Indianapolis and Can-Am competition in 1971. At Indy in 1971 Peter surprised everyone when he put his McLaren on the pole, averaging 178.696 mph and outqualifying the favored Penske McLaren of Mark Donohue. He finished second to Al Unser in the five-hundred-mile grind itself; and when the Can-Am campaign opened two weeks later at Mosport, Ontario, he was therefore much better known than before.

The untried Lola T260 was not handling well at Mosport; but Jackie Stewart's great skill enabled him to "carry the car around on his back," and he qualified fastest. He also managed to lead the race in the new car for the first half hour before a leaking transmission forced him to a stop. Denny and Peter than roared by in their M8F's to finish first and second for still another McLaren sweep.

The Lola effort of 1971 was badly handicapped, of course, in trying to develop a car in only one season that could best a team of McLarens with five years of methodical improvement behind them. Jackie did defeat the McLarens at St. Jovite (Denny had the flu there), and he passed both of the orange cars to lead at Road Atlanta until he blew a tire; but the T260 continued to handle badly throughout the season.

Peter won his first Can-Am at Road Atlanta; and

Peter Revson's first Can-Am victory came at the rolling Road Atlanta, Georgia, course in July, 1971.

then made it two in a row at Watkins Glen after Jackie lost first place again with more tire trouble. It was also at the Glen that Peter received his "Champagne Peter" name for dousing the spectators.

Jackie and the chunky Lola won on the tight and rough course at Mid-Ohio in August, but only after both team McLarens were eliminated by breaking drive shafts that turn the rear wheels. Denny's went on the first turn of the first lap, and Peter's only eight laps from the end while he held a sizable lead over Jackie.

Denny took the pole at Elkhart Lake; but Peter started from the very last position on the grid because he had not been there to qualify. (The McLaren team had divided their forces to meet a busy schedule, Peter being at Ontario, California, to qualify for an important track race.) Although Denny made a good start in Indiana, both he and Stewart were out of the race by the halfway point with mechanical failures. Meanwhile, Peter had knifed past a dozen cars on the first lap alone and kept rapidly charging through the field as the race progressed. By the time Denny had to quit, Peter was right there in his mirror, ready to take over and win the race.

After an easy victory for Peter at Brainerd, Minnesota, and Denny's win from Jackie at Edmonton when the Lola's rear suspension broke, the next race on the

1971 schedule was at Laguna Seca, California. Leading comfortably from the start, Peter seemed assured of another victory there.

Then, suddenly, just a few laps from the end of the race, his M8F began to trail heavy blue smoke from its engine. As Peter crossed the start-finish line to begin his last lap, a black flag was waved at him, signaling him to stop in case his car was dropping oil and making the course slippery. Peter did not even slow down (afterwards he said that he had not seen the flag, and it is true that the sun was in his eyes); and when he completed what should have been the last lap of the race, he received the black flag again instead of the checkered.

Around the course he smoked for an extra lap with second-place Jackie Stewart still attempting to close the gap. As they approached the start-finish line once more in the most confusing finish of the Can-Am series, the starter still did not give the checkered flag to Peter but waved it at Jackie instead. The arguments and protests began immediately afterward. After much heated discussion and the discovery that the M8F was leaking oil only very slightly, Peter was eventually declared the winner over Stewart. He was also fined $250 for ignoring the black flag.

Riverside is the last, richest and most prestigious of the Can-Am races; and in 1971 it also decided the

Can-Am championship between Denny and Peter. Denny took the first grid position and Peter the second; then the pair finished the race in the same order, neither of them putting a wheel wrong for two hundred demanding miles.

Added to the points for his five previous wins in

His five victories in 1971 made Peter Revson the first American Can-Am champion.

1971, Peter's second at Riverside was enough to make him the first American Can-Am champion. Denny was second in overall points and Jackie third.

Forty-nine races have now been run in the first six years of the series and Team McLaren sports/racers have won thirty-seven of them, independent McLarens accounting for two additional victories. The Orange Train has become an Orange Steamroller in the minds of many; and at the end of the 1971 season Team McLaren grew even stronger. Teddy Mayer announced that Peter Revson would be moving up to the McLaren Grand Prix team in 1972 (one of the very few Americans to compete at this level), and that former rival Jackie Stewart would join Denny to drive the all-new McLaren Can-Am M20's.

In spite of this, there are indications at the time of writing that Team McLaren may not have things entirely its own way in 1972, after all. The Lola group is said to be already testing a speedy new challenger somewhere in the south of France; and there is big news from Porsche in Germany.

Porsche, winner of the World Manufacturers' Championship for endurance sports cars the past three years, has decided to enter a full-scale factory team in the 1972 Can-Am series. They are expected to run a new sports/racer based on the extremely reliable twelve-cylinder 917 that has won such famous endurance races as Le Mans, the Targa Florio and Sebring. Furthermore, the Can-Am Porsche is said to have the first turbocharged engine in Can-Am history. (A turbocharged engine is one that uses its own exhaust gasses to operate a special pump that pushes a larger amount of fuel mixture into the cylinders than usual, thereby producing much more power.)

Not only is the strong Porsche factory racing organization coming into the Can-Am, their team will be managed by the efficient Roger Penske and its number one driver is to be Mark Donohue. If ever the mighty McLarens are to be beaten for the Can-Am championship, the Porsche-Penske-Donohue team seems the most likely contender to many experts.

But regardless of the particular car that wins a Can-Am event or the driver behind its wheel, many thousands of fans thrill to the noise, color and blazing speed of each race. The big unlimited cars and their glittering international teams have become the favorites of many road-racing enthusiasts in the United States and Canada; and they are likely to be attracting record crowds for many exciting seasons to come.